T0327892

From Scandinavia:

Graphic design from Scandinavia, compiled and published by Counter-Print

First published in 2017 © Counter-Print
Reprinted in 2018, 2020
ISBN 978-0-9935812-2-9 Designed by Jon Dowling & Céline Leterme
www.counter-print.co.uk

With special thanks to all the contributors.

Design and Scandinavia: two words which have become synonymous with one another and an area recognised, the world over, for its ability to produce the kind of design we all aspire to. Truly great design, that is both functional and beautiful. This was what attracted me to visit Scandinavia exactly ten years ago and, with the anniversary of my trip being the impetus for this book, further exploration into the relationship between a geographic location and its creative output.

What struck me from my travels to Scandinavia, absorbing life on a daily basis, was the focus put into the design of common everyday touch-points. Whether holding a Scandinavian product in one's hand or experiencing a private or public space, I found the quality and concern for ergonomics, functionality and sustainability inspiring: I have kept a disposable set of wooden cutlery, beautifully crafted, that I haven't been able to bring myself to use yet, that stands testament to this.

In the intervening years since my first trip to this area and the making of this book, Scandinavian style and creativity seems to have infiltrated every area of life. From television programs in the shape of Nordic noir, fashion with stores such as Acne and Cos and cuisine, with NOMA celebrating locality and seasonality in the culinary experience. The trend for all things Scandinavian has never been stronger.

The Scandinavian graphic design within this book emanates from the same roots as all Scandinavian design. In ancient times, the harsh conditions of the Nordic countries meant that most implements needed to sustain life had primarily to work and to last. Time was spent mostly in earning a living and there was limited time or need for decoration. The Scandinavian shorthand for beauty became that of simplicity and functionality, with designs for homeware and furniture based on bare, simple forms – a sparse visual narrative that remains prevalent in work from this area to this day.

Every culture reflects its beliefs, values and attitudes in their design. Scandinavian design is seen as democratic, functional and simple, or as the famous Swedish graphic designer Olle Eksell titled his book, 'Design = Economy'. The creative output from this area exemplifies the same characteristics now as in the 1950s heyday of Nordic design, when furniture and homeware designers of this period, such as Alvar Aalto, Arne Jacobsen, Borge Mogensen, Marimekko, Verner Panton and Iittala garnered international praise. →

Perhaps less well known, but of equal importance, was the work of Scandinavian graphic designers and illustrators at this time. Designers such as Anders Beckman, Tapani Aartomaa, Martti Mykkänen, Arne Ungermann, Stig Lindberg, Olle Eksell and John Melin also pioneered a Scandinavian aesthetic and helped influence subsequent generations of designers in their field.

It may be over half a century since the 1950's heyday, but as you will see in this book Scandinavian designers are still taking on the legendary reputations of their predecessors, exploring, building upon and even challenging the conventions of their legacy.

The importance of design is clearly taken very seriously in Scandinavia, with a solid infrastructure well placed to capitalise on young Scandinavian talent. Investment in education, with higher education largely being free, has resulted in Scandinavia boasting some of the best design schools in the world, such as the Bergen Academy of Art and Design in Norway, Finland's Aalto University and Konstfack University in Sweden. Svensk Form in Sweden demonstrates the benefits of good design for social development and The Danish Design Center highlights the value of design for Denmark-based businesses. The Iceland Design Centre organises lectures and exhibitions and facilitates collaboration between local designers and artists, while The Norwegian Design Council promotes design as a strategic tool for innovation.

Such belief and commitment to the benefits of good design has resulted in 'Scandinavian design' becoming acknowledged as a byword for quality and the investment in this area is surely something the rest of the world could learn from.

Jon Dowling
Counter-Print

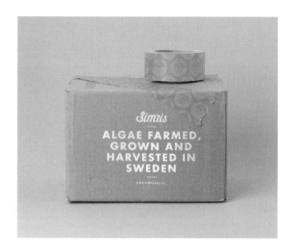

Simris
Food and health brand who make
products from algae
2015

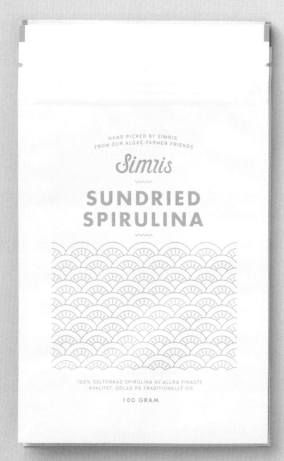

**TUSEN TACK!
HÄR KOMMER DINA
ALGER. HOPPAS
DU GILLAR DEM!**

WWW.SIMRISALG.SE · WWW.FACEBOOK.COM/SIMRISALG

SIMRIS ALG AB
ALGAE FARMED, GROWN & HARVESTED IN SWEDEN
Herrestadsvägen 24A · 276 50 Hammenhög, Sweden
www.simrisalg.se

Target

Social media campaign for
a commercial retail chain
2015

Häng Konsten Lågt
Book design for a writer & artist
2015

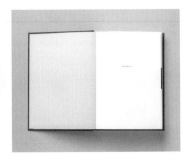

Kontroll

Book design for a writer & artist
2014

→

Malmö Festival 2014

Experiencial design for
Scandinavia's largest city festival
2014

MALMÖ
FESTIVALEN
~FIRAR~
30 ÅR!
15-22 augusti
Gratis FÖR ALLA
PUSS & KRAM

Malmö stad

Scandic

Läs mer om festivalen och programmet
på vår hemsida → WWW.MALMOFESTIVALEN.SE

←

Malmö Festival 2014

Poster design for Scandinavia's
largest city festival
2014

Hemslöjden

Branding for the National
Association of Swedish Handicraft
2014

Washington Post Magazine

Cover design for a special
lifestyle edition
2015

iNatur
Skinca

Conta
(extra
20 mg

185 ml/6.2 fl.oz.
Made in Australia

is

185 ml/6.2 fl.oz.
Made in Australia

Bedow

bedow.se

iNature Skincare

Packaging for an Australian
manufacturer of natural skincare
products free from parabens,
artificial colors and fragrances
2013

→

Erik Penser Bank

Book design for Sweden's leading
private bank
2011

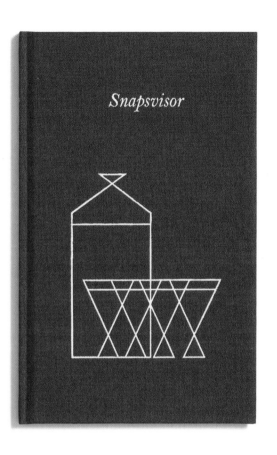

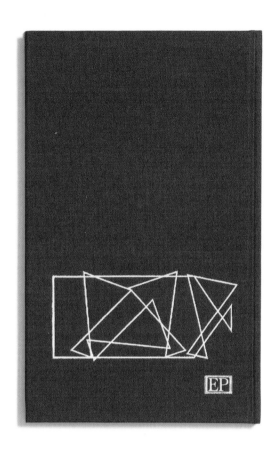

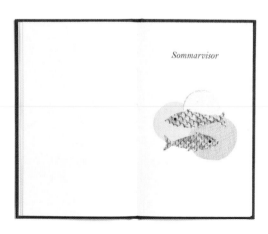

Biggans Böcklingpastej

Fish paste packaging

2013

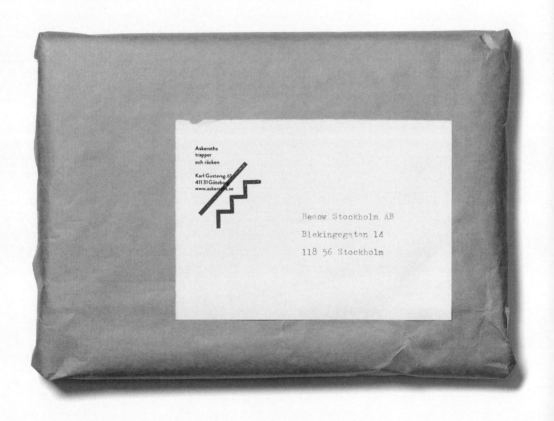

Askeroths Trappor Och Räcken

Branding for a manufacturer
of stairs & railings
2013

Bielke & Yang

bielkeyang.com

Holzweiler Agency
Branding for one of Norway's
largest fashion brand distributors
2013

Grafill
Bielke+Yang
Colophon Foundr
Black AaBb

Visuelt

Visual profile for Scandinavia's
largest annual event within visual
communication
2014

Oslo Design Fair
Visual identity for Norway's
oldest & biggest home furnishing
trade show
2015

Illustration
Magnus Voll Mathiassen

Photography
Calle Huth

Bielke & Yang

Oslo Design Fair
___

Visual identity for Norway's
oldest & biggest home furnishing
trade show
2015

Illustration

Magnus Voll Mathiassen

Photography

Calle Huth

Solrug

Packaging design for Finnish rye bread
2015

Illustration

Rami Niemi

Bond

bond-agency.com

Moomin
Brand guidelines for packaging
2014

WAASTAA

Branding for a visual directory
for creatives
2014

→

Ainoa

Shopping mall identity
2014

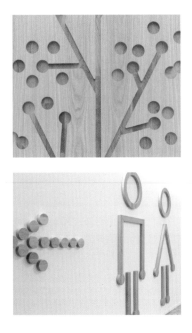

Hopeatoffee for Cloetta

Packaging design for confectionery
2014

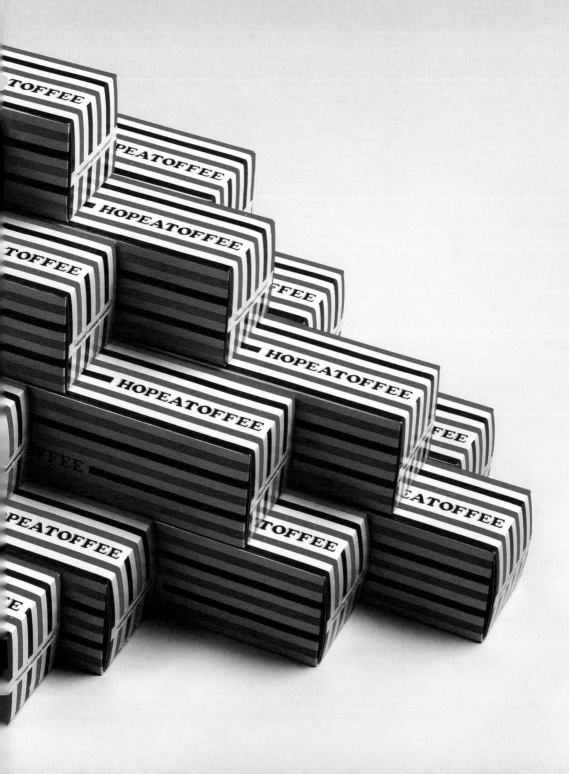

Allsorts for Cloetta

Packaging design for confectionery
2013

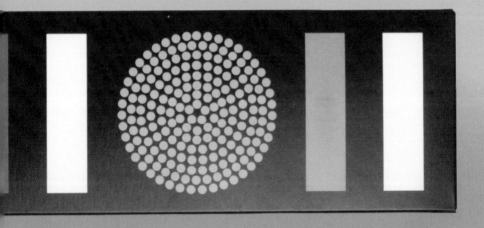

Puustelli Miinus
Branding for a kitchen
manufacturer
2014

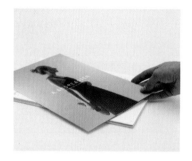

A. Andreassen

Branding for a lifestyle brand

2016

BVD

bvd.se

Modern Times Group MTG
Branding for a media group
2014

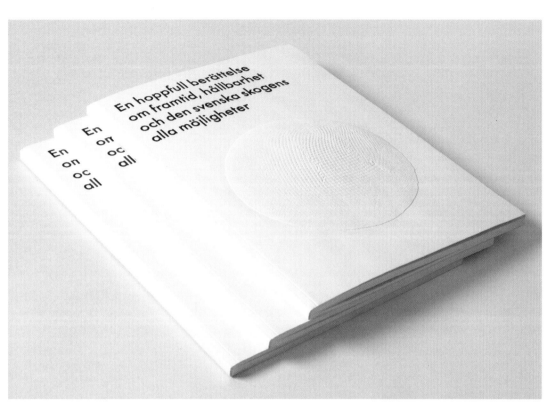

Skogsindustrierna

Book design for The Swedish Forest
Industries Federation
2015

Skandia Banken
Wayfinding & experiencial design
for a bank
2009

→

Apotek Hjärtat
Brand identity for a Swedish
pharmacy store
2009

Stockholmsmässan

Exhibition design for Formex
2012

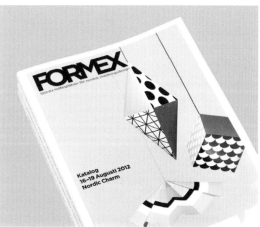

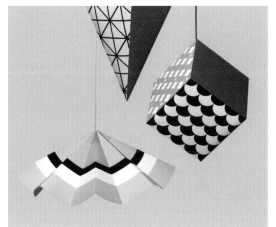

Beckers Scotte for Tikkurila
Sweden AB
Packaging design for professional
painting products
2012

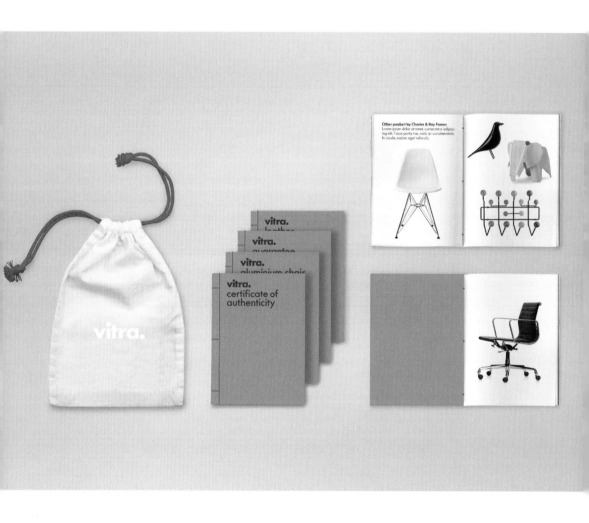

Vitra
Packaging design & retail
environment for a furniture
company
2012

Vitra
Packaging design & retail
environment for a furniture
company
2012

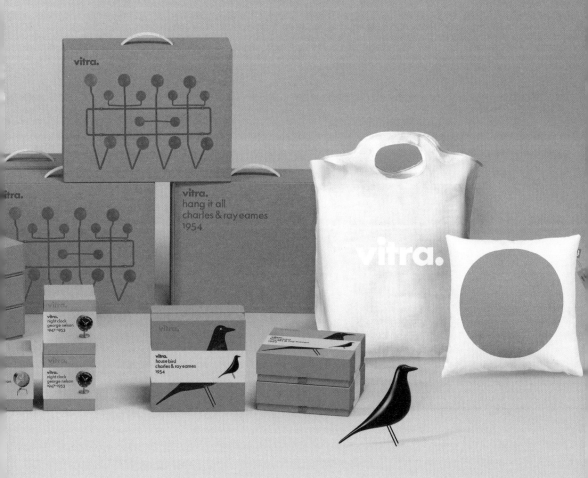

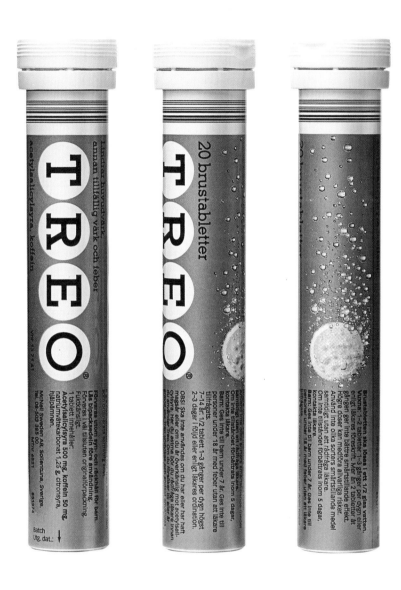

Treo
—
Packaging design for
pharmaceutical products
2008

7-Eleven
Packaging & interior design
for a coffee convenience store
2011

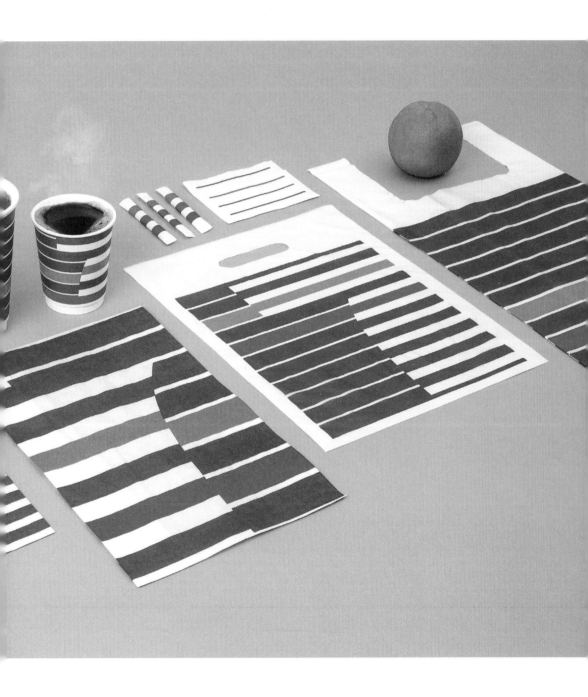

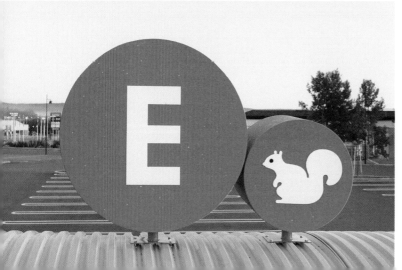

Ingelsta shopping for
Eurocommercial Properties
Signage & experiencial design
for a shopping mall in Sweden
2008

Heydays

heydays.no

KK Wind Solutions®

HQ   KK Wind Solutions A/S   Phone   +45 97 22 10 33   E-mail   main@kkwindsolutions.com
     Bøgildvej 3   Fax   +45 97 21 14 31   Web   www.kkwindsolutions.com
     DK-7430 Ikast   CVR   25 74 67 17

KK Wind Solutions

Branding for a wind energy
solutions company
2014

Nöra
Bogaert 107,
São Paulo, Brasil

NÖRA

Nöra

Branding for an architecture
consultancy
2013

Mellbye
—
Branding for an architecture
& interior company
2012

Sjemmedal
Branding for a housing contractor
2013

Kurppa Hosk

kurppahosk.com

Blippsy

Branding for a technology company

2015

→
Designtorget
Branding for a retail company
2015

Stol

Frankfurt
795:-

Månadens designer

Stilrent och e...
serien Gusta...
serie med ...
upplägge...
både ...
lis...

Home of
Swedish design

Look for your closest store at designtorget.se
or shop on-line.

DF Designtorget

DF

Skandinavisk
design handlar
om att göra
det härligt med
enkla medel

Dear Kurppa Hosk,

Cid qui sunt, cusciis parci id est, apero tem et volore illanda ndiorem ut
ea voluptatur sequam quis et ulparum liquid mo min nonseri onsequa te-
modit atemped mi, qui dia nulluptius vel in nobisimusdae volorib usdam.
voluptatia sequiam quaepero quod aliquatur, que res ullent a volecat
emquis del mos nonsece ssitio im enda poria sum re, odiscidero torem
que re videruptaqui des es eossimpore voluptatiam, voluptur? Quia vol-
lupt atibus essita int magnis dunt. Dam nonsed gentio est volorra epe-
dsint Quas dia volorem siminis re voluptae peratur aliquiam reptas eum
autate cor as necto et arum sum ipsam quodtbas qui conseque vendi
nos modistatus volore sae nate esci nullore mporumqui qui aditae mod
explabo. Borion re mod et utest eaquia aboreperum aut que con eos et
quis mo blam dolorem. Aquam sinis mint autecer ioned qui aclaspe rovidit
taepis et aliquis volore audit alias. BusOtas porlorest, qui aligend ebitatusaes
aut aa nimus amus restiandit velquis eum ut laccab ipsaperibus assum
sunti odicia que eum, ent od que con eos ad abori dollit
aut ut re illo ma volest occoptatur samus.
munti toremquam aut laccab ipsaperibus samus
aus Rat re illo ma volest occoptatur utem inulies eum
lis dem quas eiction utem quas quatiist, occus aci
llacc usdaese quatiist, occus aci

DF

Design

Penglot
Branding for a bank
2014

Korshags

Visual identity for a food
manufacturer
2014

Korshags
Visual identity for a food
manufacturer
2014

Larssen
& Amaral

larssenamaral.no

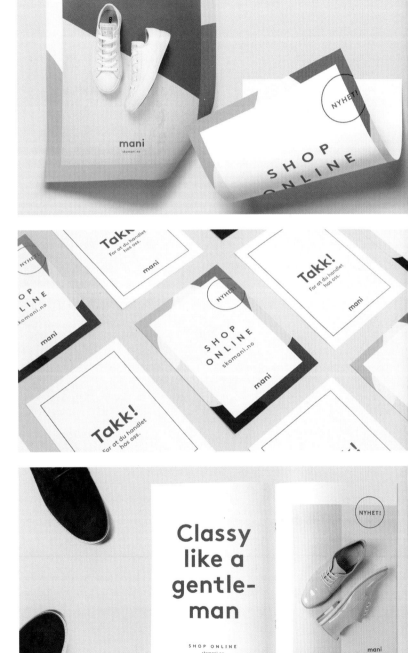

Mani
Launch campaign for a shoe shop
2016

Qvalis
Visual identity for a fitness brand
2016

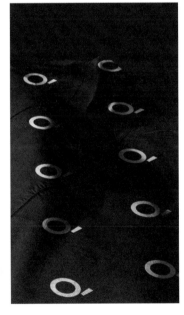

World Children's Festival
Visual identity for an educational
& cultural festival
2015

World Children's Festival

Visual identity for an educational
& cultural festival
2015

Lundgren
+Lindqvist

lundgrenlindqvist.se

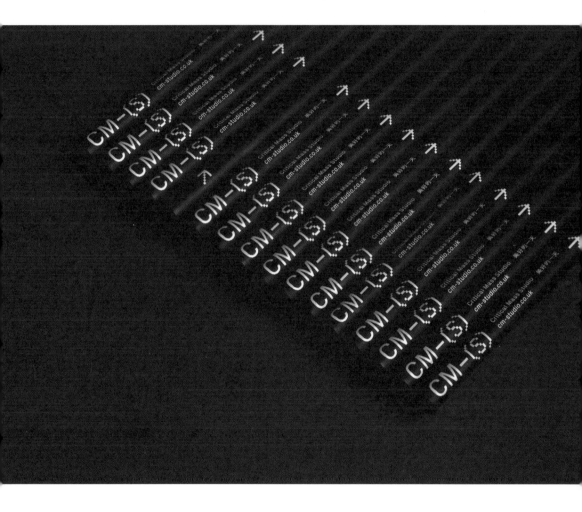

Edouard Malingue Gallery

Visual identity for a contemporary
art gallery
2015

Edouard Malingue Gallery

Visual identity for a contemporary
art gallery
2015

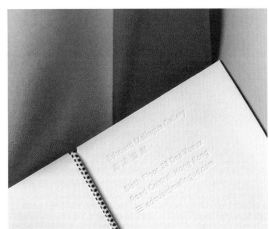

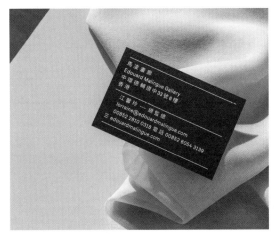

Ever Rêve
Look book design for
womenswear brand
2016

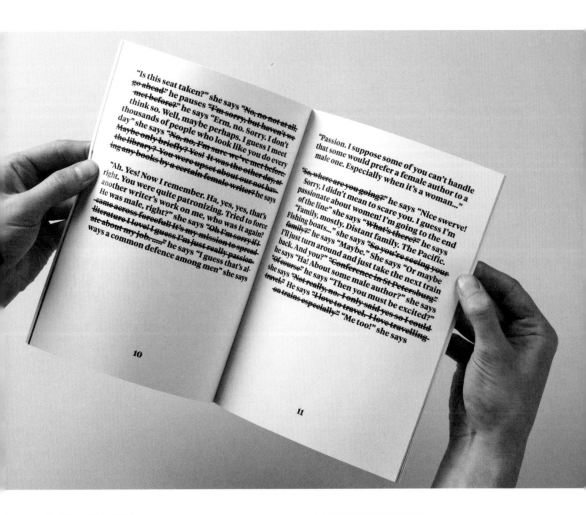

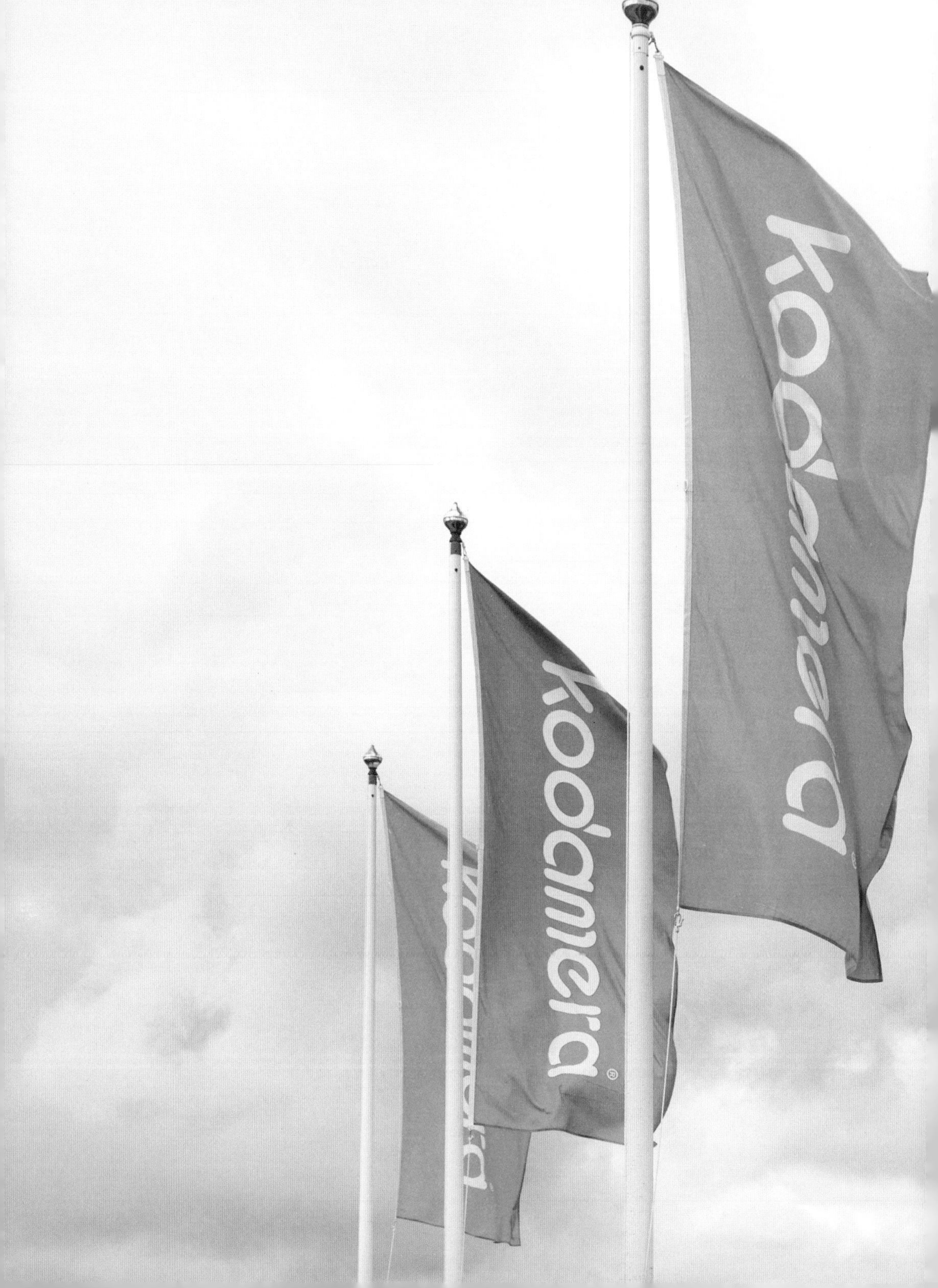

<u>Kodamera</u>
Logo design for a digital agency
2013

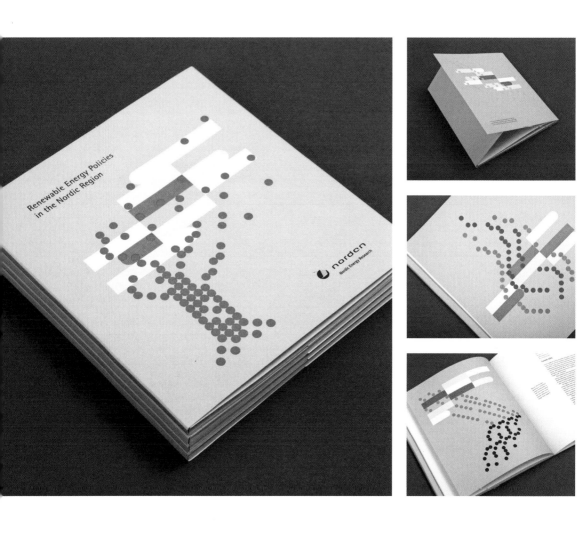

Nordic Energy Research

Book design for a platform for
cooperative energy research
& policy development
2013

Oskar Kullander
Branding for a photographer
2011

Elvine
———
Visual identity for a fashion brand
2013—2015

Scandinavian Design Group

sdg.no

TV2
Visual identity for the largest
commercial television station
in Norway
2012

Blossa 13 for Altia Sweden AB

Packaging design for an
alcoholic beverage
2012

Blossa 15 for Altia Sweden AB

Packaging design for an
alcoholic beverage
2014

Rom & Tonik

Identity for a company creating
sound absorbing wool elements
for work spaces
2014

Kalles Kaviar for Orkla Foods Sweden AB

Packaging design for food product

2015

The Studio

the-studio.se

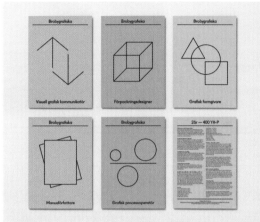

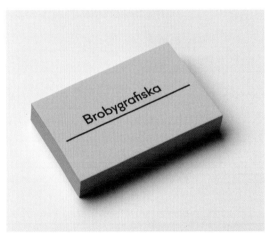

Brobygrafiska

Visual identity for a design college
2014

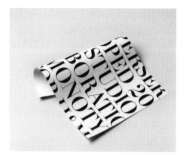

H&M Typography

Custom typeface design of HM
Amperserif for a global fashion chain
2014

Bearleader Chronicle

Brand identity for an online
travel blog
2014

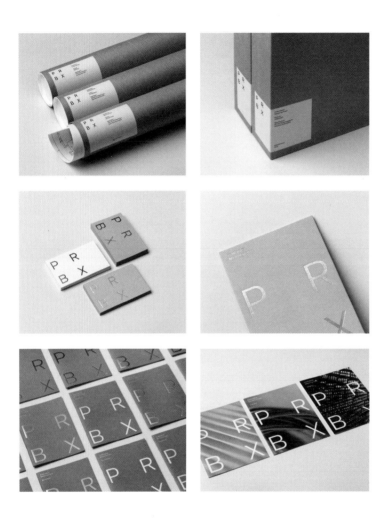

Powerbox
———
Brand identity for a company
specialising in heavy industry
power conversion
2014

Verso Skincare

Brand identity, packaging, print,
photography, retail & web design
for a global skincare brand
2013

Vete-Katten

Concept and re-brand, design program, packaging, print, photography, in-store signage & web design for a café
2015

Lemonaid.
Drinking helps.

Organic lime lemonade
with fresh pressed juice
from Fairtrade orgins.
Every sip makes our
world a little bit better.

Ingredients: Water, organic
lime juice* (10%), organic
sugar cane*, carbonic acid.
*100% of the ingredients
are from Fairtrade sources
(not including water).
Ingredienser: Vand, økologisk
lime juice* (10%), økologisk

Ingredients: Water, organic
lime juice* (10%), organic
sugar cane*, carbonic acid.
*100% of the ingredients
are from Fairtrade sources
(not including water).
Ingredienser: Vand, økologisk
lime juice* (10%), økologisk

rørsukker*, kulsyre. *Fairtrade
andelen udgør 100% (juice
taget vandet). Ingrediener:
Vatten, ekologisk limejuie*
(10%), ekologisk rörsocker*,
kolsyra. *Andelen Fairtrade
utgör 100% (förutom vatten

Best before: see cap
330 ml, please recycle.

LemonAid Beverages GmbH
Brückwiesenstraße 10
22453 Hamburg
Germany
www.lemonaid-drinks.com

DE-012-Öko-Kontrollstelle
More info on Fairtrade:
www.fairtrade.net

Lemonaid
———
Brand identity & packaging
design for a beverage brand
2013

Re-public

re-public.com

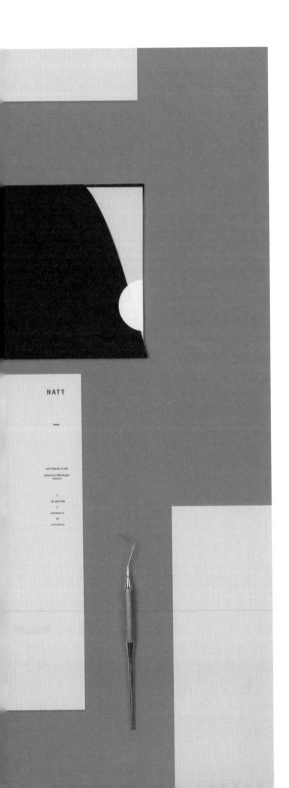

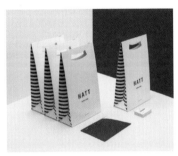

HATT
Branding for a dental clinic & spa
2015

→
Ipsen & Co
Branding for a café
2013

Ipsen & Co
Branding for a café
2013

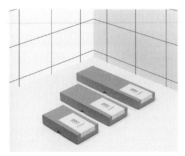

Leckerbaer
Branding for a pastry shop & café
2015

Leckerbaer
Branding for a pastry shop & café
2015

Stockholm
Design Lab

stockholmdesignlab.se

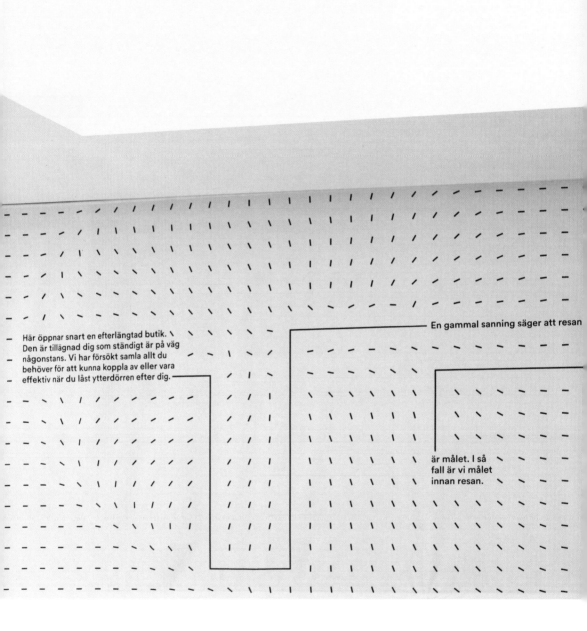

Här öppnar snart en efterlängtad butik.
Den är tillägnad dig som ständigt är på väg
någonstans. Vi har försökt samla allt du
behöver för att kunna koppla av eller vara
effektiv när du låst ytterdörren efter dig.

En gammal sanning säger att resan

är målet. I så
fall är vi målet
innan resan.

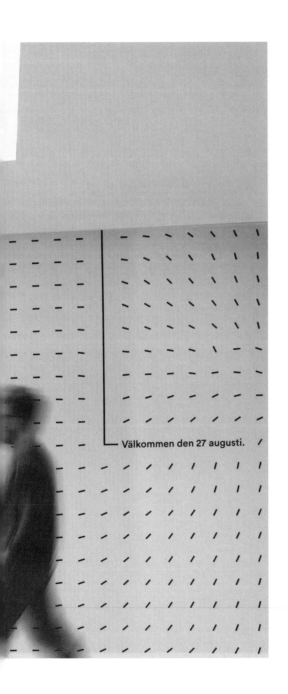

Välkommen den 27 augusti.

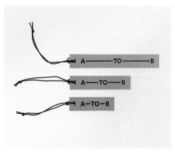

A-TO-B for Venue Retail Group

Visual identity for a shop

2015

IKEA

Packaging desing for
a furniture retailer
2005

GODIS
RÖDA SNÖREN

Candy laces with strawberry flavour /
Confiserie gélifiée à l'arôme de fraise
en forme de lacets

IKEA® FOOD   100 g

PAST
ÄLGA

IKEA FOOD

KNÄCKEBRÖD
RÅG

IKEA® FOOD

PASTEJ LAX

150 g   IKEA

TÅRTA MÖRK CHOKLAD / Almond cake with dark chocolate, quick frozen /
Mandeltorte mit Schokolade, tiefgefroren / Mandeltårta med mörk choklad, djupfry
Mantelikakku tummaa suklaata, pakaste / Ciasto migdałowo-czekoladowe, mrożon
Mandlový dort s hořkou čokoládou, hluboce zmrazený / Mandľový zákusok s čokolá
krémom, mrazený / Gyorsfagyasztott mandula torta csokoládé krémmel /
Prajitura almond cu ciocolata neagra, congelată rapid

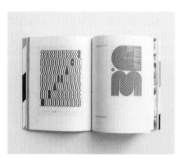

'Stripes, Rhythm, Direction'
Exhibition for Nordiska Museet
Visual identity for an exhibition
2013

Vårdapoteket

Visual identity for a pharmacy chain

2010

Åhléns
———
Visual identity for a
department store
1998

Studio Claus Due

studioclausdue.dk

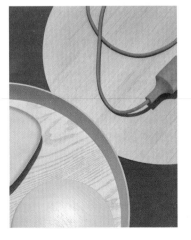

MUUTO

Catalogue design & visual
concept of campaign images
for a furniture company
2015

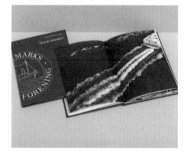

The Danish Shipowners' Association

Visual identity for The Danish
Shipowners' Association
2011

DANISH SHIPPING
Annual Logbook 2015

Danish
Shipowners'
Association

Hayward Gallery

Book design for a compilation
of exhibition posters
2013

New Carlsberg Foundation

Publication design

2013

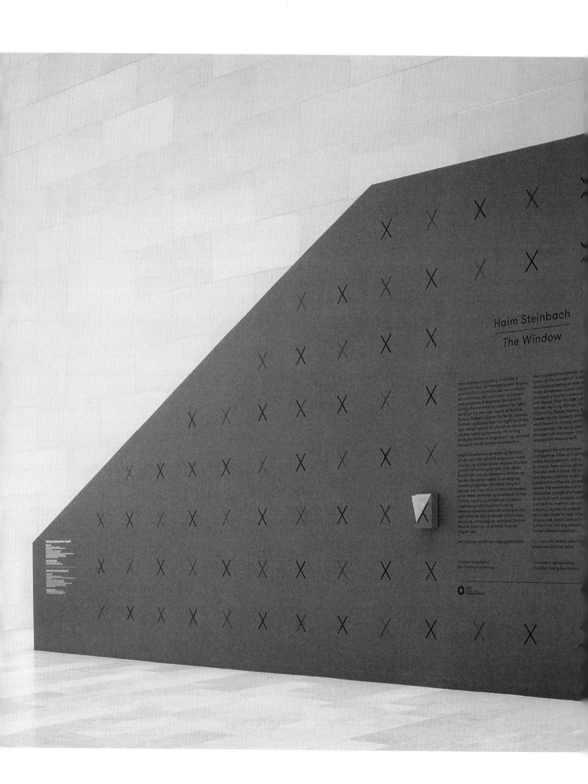

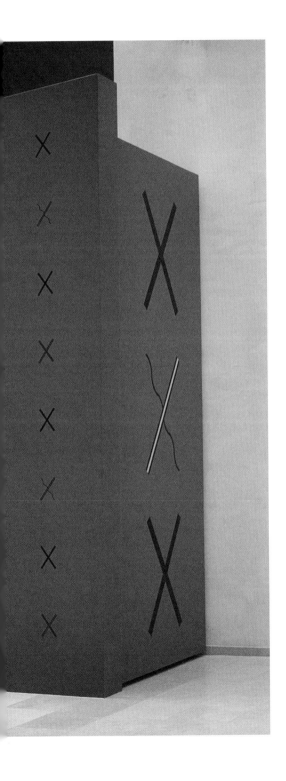

SMK, The National Gallery
of Denmark
Identity for 'x-rummet', The National
Gallery of Denmark's experimental
stage for contemporary art
2013

The Nordic Book
—
Photographic book design
of Søren Rønholt's work
2014

Janine Rewell

janinerewell.com

Fika for Isetan

Packaging design for a Japanese
department store
2015

Arla
—
Swedish food packaging
2012

MINNA
PARIKKA

Minna Parikka

Bodypaint campaign for
a luxury shoe brand
2014

MINNA
PARIKKA

MINNA
PARIKKA

MINNA
PARIKKA

Lovely Spring

Experiencial design for Lotte World
Mall, a Korean department store
2016

→
Nooks

Dollhouse design for a toy brand
2015

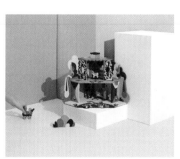

Valokki
—
Carpet design for Vm Carpet
2013

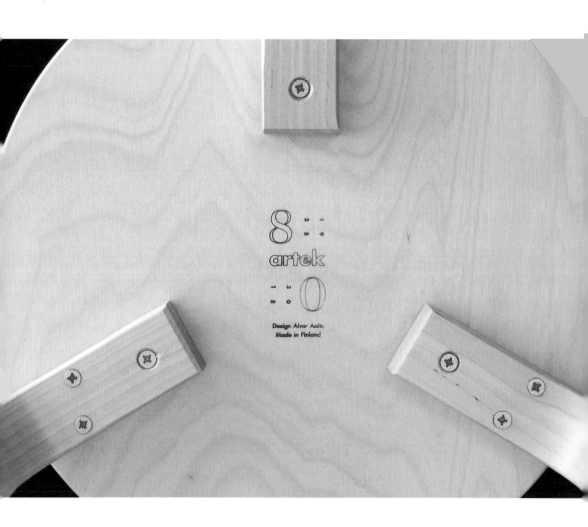

Artek 80

Visual identity for the 80th
birthday celebrations of the
furniture brand Artek
2015

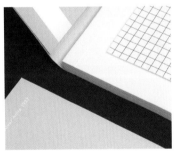

Artek 80

Design of a line of stationery
products for Artek
2015

Taidehalli

Visual identity for an art
exhibition space
2014

**Helsingin Taidehalli
Helsingfors Konsthall
Kunsthalle Helsinki**

Nervanderinkatu 3
Nervandersgatan 3
FI-00100 Helsinki / Helsingfors
+358 9 454 2060
www.taidehalli.fi

**Heidi
Kronström**

Yhteyspäällikkö   Helsingin Taidehall
Customer Service Manager   Kunsthalle Helsink
                                Nervanderinkatu 3
+358 46 7731 4316   00100 Helsinki
heidi.kronstrom@taidehalli.fi   www.taidehalli.fi

**Reetta
Haarajoki**

Viestintäpäällikkö   Helsingin Taidehal
Communications Manager   Kunsthalle Helsink
                                Nervanderinkatu
+358 40 451 4772   00100 Helsinki
reetta.haarajoki@taidehalli.fi www.taidehalli.fi

3
3
i / Helsingfors

We Are Helsinki

Editorial design for a magazine

2011

Snask snask.com
Bedow bedow.se
Bielke & Yang bielkeyang.com
Bond bond-agency.com
BVD bvd.se
Heydays heydays.no
Kurppa Hosk kurppahosk.com
Larssen & Amaral larssenamaral.no
Lundgren+Lindqvist lundgrenlindqvist.se
Scandinavian Design Group sdg.no
The Studio the-studio.se
Re-public re-public.com
Stockholm Design Lab stockholmdesignlab.se
Studio Claus Due studioclausdue.dk
Janine Rewell janinerewell.com
Tsto tsto.org